A Stew for the Crew

PHASE 5

/ew/
oe/

Level 5 – Green

Helpful Hints for Reading at Home

The graphemes (written letters) and phonemes (units of sound) used throughout this series are aligned with Letters and Sounds. This offers a consistent approach to learning whether reading at home or in the classroom.

HERE IS A LIST OF NEW GRAPHEMES FOR THIS PHASE OF LEARNING. AN EXAMPLE OF THE PRONUNCIATION CAN BE FOUND IN BRACKETS.

Phase 5			
ay (day)	ou (out)	ie (tie)	ea (eat)
oy (boy)	ir (girl)	ue (blue)	aw (saw)
wh (when)	ph (photo)	ew (new)	oe (toe)
au (Paul)	a_e (make)	e_e (these)	i_e (like)
o_e (home)	u_e (rule)		

HERE ARE SOME WORDS WHICH YOUR CHILD MAY FIND TRICKY.

Phase 5 Tricky Words			
oh	their	people	Mr
Mrs	looked	called	asked
could			

GPC focus: /ew/oe/

TOP TIPS FOR HELPING YOUR CHILD TO READ:

• Allow children time to break down unfamiliar words into units of sound and then encourage children to string these sounds together to create the word.

• Encourage your child to point out any focus phonics when they are used.

• Read through the book more than once to grow confidence.

• Ask simple questions about the text to assess understanding.

• Encourage children to use illustrations as prompts.

PHASE 5

/ew/ oe/

This book focuses on the phonemes /ew/ and /oe/ and is a green level 5 book band.

A Stew for the Crew

Written by
Shalini Vallepur

Illustrated by
Rebecca Flitcroft

"My crew will be round soon," said Sam.
"What is for tea tonight?"
"We can have mangoes and cook stew?"
said Nan.

"What sort of stew?" said Sam.
"Will the crew like a fish stew or
a chicken stew?" said Nan.

"The crew likes chicken stew. Can I help you cook it?" Sam asked.

"Yes, I need your help. Put this on, you
might get food on that top," said Nan.

"Get a big pot out," said Nan. "We will cook lots and lots of stew for the crew."

"Now we need lots of garlic. Can you peel it?" said Nan.
"It smells good!" said Sam.

Nan was chopping things to go into the stew.
"Can I chop something too?" Sam said.

"This is sharp. I will do the chopping," said Nan, as she threw peel from the potatoes into the bin.

"You can sort out the peas," said Nan.
Sam went to get the peas.

"We will need one cup of green peas to go with the stew," said Nan.

"What about the chicken?" Sam asked.
"I will cut the chicken up," said Nan.
"Can you brew some tea?"

"Put it in this mug," said Nan, picking up a blue mug. Sam threw a teabag into the blue mug.

"In goes the chicken," said Nan. The chicken went into the stew with a plop, plop, plop.

Sam could smell the stew. The smell of garlic was good.
"Yum! I cannot wait to eat it," said Sam.

"Wait!" said Sam. "Some people in my crew do not eat meat. What will we do?"

"Oh! I can cook a stew with lots of peas and beans for them," said Nan.
"Phew!" said Sam.

Sam and Nan sat down to drink tea.
"The crew will come soon," said Nan.

"You will need to get a jug, some spoons and cups and lay them out," said Nan.

"I will put a few jugs out," said Sam.
"And big pots for the stews."

"Do not forget the mangoes!" said Nan.
"And a few big spoons so I can scoop out
the stew."

Ding! Dong! Ding! Dong! The bell rang. "My crew has come!" said Sam. "I'll get it!"

"Crew! Come in Joe, Kim, Lewis and Pat!" said Sam. "Can you smell the stew?"

Joe, Kim, Lewis and Pat sat down.
"Hi, Nan! This smells so good!" said Joe.

"I cannot wait to eat this stew!" said Kim.
"Welcome, crew!" said Nan. "You can eat as much as you like."

"Did you cook this stew?" Joe asked Sam.
"This stew is the best!" said Kim.

"We have mangoes too," said Nan.
"Thanks, Nan. We did the best stew
for the crew," said Sam.

A Stew for the Crew

1. What kind of stew are Nan and Sam cooking?

    (a) Fish

    (b) Chocolate

    (c) Chicken

2. How does Sam help Nan in the kitchen?

3. What stew does Nan make for the people who don't eat meat?

4. What things go into the stew?

5. Sam and Nan love to cook food for the crew. Do you like cooking? What would you cook for your friends?

©2021 **BookLife Publishing Ltd.**
King's Lynn, Norfolk PE30 4LS

ISBN 978–1–83927–406–0

A Stew for the Crew
Written by Shalini Vallepur
Illustrated by Rebecca Flitcroft

An Introduction to BookLife Readers...

Our Readers have been specifically created in line with the London Institute of Education's approach to book banding and are phonetically decodable and ordered to support each phase of Letters and Sounds.

Each book has been created to provide the best possible reading and learning experience. Our aim is to share our love of books with children, providing both emerging readers and prolific page–turners with beautiful books that are guaranteed to provoke interest and learning, regardless of ability.

BOOK BAND GRADED using the Institute of Education's approach to levelling.

PHONETICALLY DECODABLE supporting each phase of Letters and Sounds.

EXERCISES AND QUESTIONS to offer reinforcement and to ascertain comprehension.

BEAUTIFULLY ILLUSTRATED to inspire and provoke engagement, providing a variety of styles for the reader to enjoy whilst reading through the series.

AUTHOR INSIGHT:
SHALINI VALLEPUR

Passionate about books from a very young age, Shalini Vallepur received the award of Norfolk County Scholar for her outstanding grades. Later on she read English at the University of Leicester, where she stayed to complete her Modern Literature MA. Whilst at university, Shalini volunteered as a storyteller to help children learn to read, which gave her experience and expertise in the way children pick up and retain information. She used her knowledge and her background and implemented them in the 32 books that she has written for BookLife Publishing. Shalini's writing easily takes us to different worlds, and the serenity and quality of her words are sure to captivate any child who picks up her books.

PHASE 5

/ew/
/oe/

This book focuses on the phonemes /ew/ and /oe/ and is a green level 5 book band.